How To Write A Novel

Simple Steps to Write Compelling Novels that Keep the Pages Turning

(Writing Mastery, Fiction Writing)

William Swain

Copyright Notice

Disclaimer

Reasonable care has been taken to ensure that the information presented in this book is accurate. However, the reader should understand that the information provided does not constitute legal, medical or professional advice of any kind. No Liability: this product is supplied "as is" and without warranties. All warranties, express or implied, are hereby disclaimed. Use of this product constitutes acceptance of the "No Liability" policy. If you do not agree with this policy, you are not permitted to use or distribute this product. We shall not be liable for any losses or damages whatsoever (including, without limitation, consequential loss or damage) directly or indirectly arising from the use of this product.

Can I Ask You a Quick Favor?

If you like this book, I would greatly appreciate if you could leave an honest review Reviews are very important to us authors, and it only takes a minute to post.

Download Audio

This book is also available now as an audiobook.

Head over to www.audible.com or

Download on the Audible application

Unlock Your True Writing Potential

What's holding back your writing? Take this free assessment now and learn to unlock your true potential:

https://www.subscribepage.com/novel

Table Of Contents

Contents

Introduction

This book contains simple and easy steps that could guide you in writing compelling novels that will keep your readers turning every page.

At last, this is it! You've finally decided to start writing your first novel. But you're probably wondering what you should do to get started.

Writing a novel seems like an extremely big task because it entails a lot of research and attempt until you find what works best.

There's no such thing as easy answers when writing a novel.

There's also no secret or magic formula to create a bestselling book.

All you need to know is that writing takes time and the more you write, the more things will fall into place.

Every novel is different. It has its own shape, momentum, and manner of reflecting life around you. This book will provide you with the basics and from there, you can work on the story that you've always wanted to write. You'll learn about the important aspects and elements of fiction writing that can bring your story to life and captivate your readers.

Everyone has a story to tell and believe that yours is worth sharing. Start writing and enjoy the process!

Thanks for downloading this book. I hope you enjoy it!

Chapter 1: Assembling the Essentials

Writing alone is not an easy task, let alone writing a full length novel. Time, effort and energy are needed from beginning to end to finish the work.

It would help to keep in mind that people are different. Therefore, if something works for other people, that doesn't necessarily mean that it will work for you. Writers are unique and creative in their own way, so study and discover what works best for you.

To begin your writing journey, here are a few tips to help you get started.

THE WRITER'S ROOM

Some writers may be comfortable in creating their masterpiece around a busy environment where they can gather a lot of inspiration, while others may need a quiet time to collect and organize all of their thoughts. It doesn't matter whether you belong in the former or the latter group, start by finding a room that you can tag as your own private writing space.

An ideal space would be somewhere where no one can bother you once you're in the writing zone. You don't really have to get out of the house or even rent a place; you can simply write inside your car if you want to, go to a nearby coffee shop or restaurant, or settle at a park with a little scenery.

What's important is that you're comfortable with your space and it's private enough that you can turn it into your own writing cave. Besides, if you're a writer, it should be easy for you to write anywhere; you just have to make sure that you have the tools you need.

WRITING GEARS

Writers have different means of writing. Today, there are various powerful digital writing tools that can support your work, but you shouldn't spend too much time just finding the right set up. The writing part is still the most important part of the job.

Perhaps, it would be helpful to think that back in the day, writers didn't even have personal computers and other devices to write. Writers like Shakespeare or Dickens only required a pen (or quill and ink) and paper to write their novels. The stories are much more important than the tools.

However, in today's generation, it would be wrong not to take advantage of the tools that can assist you in your writing, such as Microsoft Word or Google docs. If you're the kind of writer who is comfortable in handwriting your first draft, you can always do the typing on the computer afterwards. You can also hire someone for that job if you can afford it.

To jumpstart your work, think of everything that you'll be needing when you write. Keep them within your reach so you won't have to keep on standing up and finding things all over the place. That will only interfere with your work.

Here is a list of things you might be needing in your writing space.

Materials:

- Pens or pencils
- Notebook or pads
- Printing paper
- Writing journal
- Sticky notes
- Staplers

- Tape dispensers

- Paper clips

- Push pins

- Bulletin board

Apps:

- Grammarly. It is a software and online platform that checks grammar, spelling, and detects plagiarism when writing.

- Hemingway App. It is an online editor that emphasizes and corrects sentence structure, fluency, and grammar to help make your work better.

ARCHIVE YOUR WORK

Creating a great story is useless if don't save your work −you can't create a great story if you don't find the time to write down whatever comes to mind. Nowadays, it's extremely easy to carry with you a small or portable notebook to note down ideas that come along the way. You can even use your smartphone and install apps to record your thoughts.

Take a little time to find the best programs to create and save your work. Some of the popular tools you can use include Google Drive, Evernote, Dropbox, and Scrivener.

It's alright if you prefer to initially write your book with pen and paper. Still, it's essential to transfer your work on a computer. It will certainly be of help if you might ever lose one (physical paper) or the other (digital document). It would be a relief knowing that you have a backup.

See to it that you can easily access everything you need. That way, you'll have no excuse to skip on your writing project or get distracted.

THINGS TO REMEMBER

When writing a novel, you don't necessary have to work on it or build it up chapter by chapter. Go with the fragments. Write a simple paragraph or start by writing a single page. If there's a particular scene that comes to mind, write it.

Give yourself the freedom to start with bits and pieces. Don't force yourself to write 10,000 words in one sitting. Write a few words every day. Some writers even prefer to start writing their novel by working on the ending first.

Novel-writing is like a puzzle. Take it piece by piece until you get to see the whole picture. The most important thing is to put something on a page. Just write. You'll eventually get into the rhythm of writing.

As soon as you're done with your day's work, take some time to clean up and prepare your room for another writing day. This will help you build up the habit of always looking forward to working on a great novel.

Chapter 2: Constructing the Outline

Now that you're settled in your writing room with all the tools you need, it's time to start thinking about the main concept that you want to build up for your book. If you already have an existing idea, you can work by polishing it.

Start your brainstorming process. There are various methods for this, such as free writing, or making a list of things that seem interesting to you. Let your mind take you to a certain point or theme that might just be the greatest concept ever.

If you have a writing journal, you can take a look at it and see if there's anything you've written that can spark a fascinating idea. Your everyday thoughts may lead you into something worthwhile and worth writing about.

Once you came up with a concept for your novel, start choosing a suitable genre for your story. Is it drama? Is it suitable enough to be a thriller? Would comedy be appropriate for the idea? When you have decided on this, you can read the works of other authors who have produced great stories in that specific genre to broaden your picture.

It's good to be inspired by some many great authors throughout time, however, make sure that what you're going to write is an original. Perhaps, you might have a common concept that you could turn into an authentic piece by creating a different plot twist.

If you're already confident about your whole idea that it's enough for you to write hundreds of pages, then you're good to go. Start writing. Otherwise, keep on brainstorming.

DO SOME DIGGING—RESEARCH

Although you're writing a fiction novel, which means that everything is created from inside your head, your story still has to be believable and relatable if you want it to succeed. Everything needs to make sense, especially for your readers. If not, they're not going to turn those pages until the end.

When your premise is established, you must follow it with a logical storyline. For you to achieve this, you need to do some research. Successful research is how you can add the necessary details to make everything work out.

For instance, if you write about a character who is a lawyer, you have to learn everything about that profession. If not, you're surely going to receive negative feedback from your readers. It's all about accuracy. When you provide accurate details to your story, it enriches and adds authenticity to it. But if you present your readers with the wrong details, they'll lose interest and confidence in your entire story.

Here are some tips in doing your research:

- Seek help from a dictionary. Using a Thesaurus when writing is not a mortal sin. However, remember to keep your words simple for easy reading. Dictionaries can be useful in trying to find the right words.

- Read encyclopedias. You can visit a library or check online to access or borrow one if you don't have your own set. A lot of information can be obtained from encyclopedias.

- Check out World Almanacs if you need to verify geography, cultural norms, or find names suited for your characters, especially when your story is established in a specific setting or period. For instance, a certain gesture might mean different for various cultures.

- Take advantage of search engines or watch YouTube videos. You'll surely get a heap of results that you can find helpful in writing.

- Consider interviewing people. Nothing beats details that come directly from experts. People love talking about themselves and what they do. A simple conversation can give you a variety of ideas.

Don't skimp on the research part. There will be readers who will try to correct you if they read something that seems off. Fiction or fantasy stories require credibility no matter what kind of universe you create.

In doing your research, be careful not to put every fact you've learned in your story. Don't try to impress your readers with your research.

Instead, make it a means of enriching their reading experience.

CREATE AN OUTLINE

Sometimes, you might be lost in the chaos of your thoughts. There may be so many ideas running through your head. Don't rush. Give yourself some time to go over your ideas until a specific thought catches your attention because it's something that you definitely would like to read. Choose something that you're passionate about.

A great concept is one that you can't stop thinking about. That alone can give you enough reason to sit down and write your story.

When it comes to creating an outline, there is no right or wrong way of doing it. Do what works for you. You can lay down all the details before writing or you can simply go with the flow.

Some writers are outliners. An outliner is someone who chooses to plot the details before he starts writing. If you're keen to understand your characters and the situations they're in right from the start up until the very end, then you're most likely an outliner.

On the contrary, there are writers who are pantsers. A pantser is someone who starts writing with an idea in mind and then continues by following the path towards discovery.

Use an approach that feels very natural and relaxed. In some cases, they can be mixed together—creating an outline and allowing the story to progress on its own. Do what is most sensible to you.

You need to place much importance on this step. Otherwise, it would be difficult for you to come up with a clear and logical narrative. You don't want to lose the message of your story.

THE METHODS

There are different methods in creating an outline for your novel. You can divide your book into chapters or create sections that can be broken down into chapters. You can list the highlights or the main points of each chapter before writing the entire content.

You can also make use of a whiteboard or cork board and pin your ideas so you can have a visual breakdown of the content of your novel. Don't be afraid to experiment. Just find a method that suits you best.

FILL IN THE GAPS

It's possible that your initial outline might have some gaps. Fill them in by thinking about the things that make a story great. Storytelling requires an excellent blueprint.

You may already have a character that has a problem, a great setting, a perfect villain or maybe an obstacle to overcome. What's next? It's now time to ponder on the main things that your readers need to stay hooked and continue on turning those pages.

- It needs to display tension.

- It needs to be reasonable.

- It needs a heart.

There are various ways to find those holes in your outline, such as putting some setups, as well as payoffs. If you have a particular scene somewhere near the ending that needs an explanation, check to see if you have an earlier scene that clears up everything. For instance, if your character is a soldier who hacks computers at the end, you need to establish in the earlier part of your story why he can do such a thing like that.

Writers have different ways of breaking the chapters of their books, which also creates several outcomes. Some novels have a few short chapters while others have a few big chapters. There are also writers who prefer to write their stories without chapter breaks.

If you're going to have some chapter breaks, you have to place them deliberately. Don't allow yourself to get confused on how to separate your plot points and turn them into chapters. Simply create your first draft of the novel. You can think about your chapter breaks on the revision stage.

Yet, when you're thinking about your storyline and along the way there are certain chapter breaks that stirs up your imagination and creativity, take note of them. Write them down so you can go about creating an outline that includes those chapter breaks.

Write down every new scene that comes to mind. Make some notes. This can be a good way to support your outline. If you ever get overwhelmed by a mountain of ideas, ask yourself, "What is the heart of my story?" Think about why you dreamt of writing this particular story.

An outline can give you a sense of direction when you write a novel. The only thing that can be of a disadvantage is that it provides your novel with certain limitations on so many possibilities. You can get stuck. To make it work, create an outline for at least a few pages of your story and then see where it takes you.

Chapter 3: Building Setting

In the world of film and photography, it's easy to take in the visuals we see right in front of our eyes. In novels, in takes imagination to see the world form through words. Nevertheless, we can see how powerful visuals can be as a part of the story element.

It's extremely important to make your setting blend perfectly into the story you're trying to create, whether you make use of the real world or create an alternate universe.

When considering the setting for your novel-writing, it's quite obvious to think about where you want the story to take place. But this element is not just about the where, but also about the what, when, why and how questions.

A story setting must be specific. If you introduce a city, consider the part, the street, the building and the reason the story takes place there.

THE ELEMENTS

- Location. A story doesn't necessarily have to happen in a normal setting. You can take it on a desert, under the sea, or in the outer space. You should be able to describe it to make the readers feel like the place is familiar to them. Think about the emotions you want to trigger or the image you want them to see in their minds. Lay down the things your character sees. Bring everything to life.

- Occupation. It may seem unnecessary at first but this provides a sense of place. Your character may be a doctor or a lawyer and knowing what they do can help the readers see more clearly the world in which they're a part of. Describe what the hospital or office looks like.

Consider creating an engrossing backdrop.

- History and Tradition. Add a dimension by including several events in your setting, such as fairs and carnivals. You can write about how a town celebrates big events or how they treat foreigners in their town. You can even make something up since you're writing a fiction novel. Highlight a custom or social occasion that can make your setting unique.

- Historical Period. This only applies to you if your story is set decades or centuries ago. It's important to get all the facts straight. Many of your readers might be major fans of history. Check your details. There might be things we have now that doesn't exist in the past. Again, do some research.

- Humanize the Setting. If you're going to mention something about a house or maybe a street, don't just write about them in a lifeless kind of way. Add a little bit of character or soul to them. For instance, you can say that the house is your character's greatest treasure because it was a family inheritance or the street is blocked because it is cursed—accidents always happen when people try to pass through.

USING SETTING TO IMPROVE THE STORY

Writers know that the setting is an important aspect of a story. In cinema, it's an enriching experience for the audience when filmmakers immerse them in an entirely different world. For writers, it also serves as a remarkably powerful tool.

Hook the Readers

Fiction-writing is really about taking your readers to a new place, enough to make them forget everything around them. If you want to accomplish this as a writer, you have to master the setting.

Build a strong foundation of your imaginary reality right from the first part of your story. Interesting characters and well-established plots can capture the full attention of a reader—getting them to observe everything that is presented to them. However, an excellent setting is one that allows the readers to actively participate in the whole story.

There are two things you need to make readers feel like they just stepped inside your own world—a captivating setting and powerful picture of locations.

Impart a More Profound Meaning

Setting alone doesn't make a great story, but it intensifies all other story elements like the theme, mood, and plot.

It adds a deeper and more meaningful concept that stays in the minds of the readers even after they set aside the book. You establish something special and even magical deep within them.

Impart a More Intense Emotion

You may be already familiar with common but effective images like a broken-hearted character alone under the rain. When a character feels miserable, they are still given a fine day in the middle of their sorrowful feelings.

Use setting as one of your main tools to establish the mood of the scenes. Sometimes, readers would no longer spot the common choices you make when they're already hooked with the characters and the plot.

Search For Various Levels of Setting

Keep on exploring several levels and go deeper in the setting to make your story more captivating. For instance, place your character on a beach in Hawaii, waiting for the sun to set while riding on his surfboard.

You can always add new things to get the readers to know and understand further the world of your main character. Your story can transpire in one location, but the setting makes every scene entirely different. Create an atmosphere that fits your story perfectly. Choose whatever works best.

Don't Just Settle With Descriptive Paragraphs

Many ideas usually come up when you're writing a novel, but don't just write what you think. Establishing a setting can be done through any other means, not just description alone. You can relay the kind of atmosphere you want to build in so many ways.

One way to construct the setting is by using dialogue. Think about the way your characters and the people around them talk in every area. Maybe they have accents or they talk in a formal manner. Do they speak in a certain language that no one on Earth can understand?

You can create a rich and abundant world without writing so many descriptive paragraphs. Look for ways to form setting by working on different elements.

Find the Perfect Time to Concentrate on Setting

Setting runs steady throughout your whole story. The characters you create exists in a particular place or time. But don't make setting the primary focus of every scene. You might overdo it. There's a right time to convey it.

Always Think About the Readers

Aside from heightening the reading experience through moods and the plot, setting is useful to inform your readers where your characters are.

Don't let your readers to get lost in the middle of the story. Make sure they can keep up with the character's entire journey, especially when the story jumps from one scene to another.

When a character goes to another location—no matter what part of the scene he is—provide a description for the new setting so as not to get your readers completely disoriented while trying to follow the character's story.

Edit Out What's Unnecessary

Even in writing, "less is more" applies to setting. If the character moves from one location to another in every scene, that will make your readers uncomfortable.

This doesn't necessarily mean that you can't write or add several different locations. You just have to consider whether or not a location is truly needed on your story. Don't put too much stuff but don't cut too much as well.

Like other elements in a story, setting must only enhance the readers' experience. When you add a new location, it must bring something new to the story. Otherwise, you can simply use an existing location to add details to your character's life.

Provide the Basics

Every writer doesn't want their readers to feel lost when reading their novel. If you want to achieve the same thing, you need to supply the basics so they have something to grasp in the scene. The only exception would be if the character really feels lost in a particular scene, then you can give the readers the same feeling as well.

A good example would be to specify that if the character is inside a coffee shop, that shop is only a couple of blocks away from his house. Align it with a location that the readers already know.

An extent of location would also be a good idea. For instance, is the coffee shop at the corner of the street or in between houses or buildings? Give something definite to make it a lot easier for readers to comprehend what is happening.

Explore the Details

As a writer, there are many things you can learn or discover just by looking at the world around you. Are you running out of fascinating details to write for your novel? Step outside of your writing room for a while and see the world that's out there. There might be a handful of interesting things you've never seen before.

Use your five senses when exploring your surroundings. That will help you bring life to what you write.

Chapter 4: Choosing the Point of View

Who will tell the story? Will it be from the point of view of the main character? Is there a narrator who can jump into the character's thoughts from time to time? Or will it be told on a third person point of view that follows the journey of a character throughout your novel?

Choosing a perspective can be tricky at times because there's so much that it encloses. When writing a novel, it's the point of view that can influence the structure and feel of the entire story.

WHAT YOU NEED TO UNDERSTAND

Considering the right point of view only boils down to two things:

- The voice. First person using I, me; Second person using you, your; Third person using he, she, it, they

- Your character's standpoint. Think about to whom the story belongs to.

Ideally, the fundamental rule in writing a novel is to only use one perspective per chapter or preferably, for the entire story. Don't switch from one character's point of view to another within the same sentence, paragraph, or scene. It will only confuse the readers.

Many amateur writers make this a common mistake. But establishing the point of view is too important that you really have to give some thoughts to it and work on it.

Think about the story's point of view like its own camera. In film, you instantly know what viewpoint storytellers use when you watch the final cut. That's generally the same when writing a novel.

For instance, when you use a first person viewpoint, it is through the character's perspective that readers get to experience everything. They see what the character sees, hear what the character hears, or taste what the character tastes in the story. The readers don't have to hop into someone else's head.

Novels are usually written in the third person point of view because for some writers, using the first person is very limiting, but it's really not. When you want to restrain yourself from jumping into different perspective, then the first person would make this easy for you.

If you want to further familiarize yourself in using any of these viewpoints, it's best to read some latest, best-selling novels to have an idea on how renowned authors do it.

THE BREAK DOWN

Now it's time to have a closer look on each point of view.

The First Person Point of View

The main character is the one who narrates the story in this point of view. It is commonly used in fiction-writing, next to the third person.

If you're a beginner, this is highly recommended since it limits you to a single perspective—although this is really the proper way of writing the story, except when you opt for an omniscient fictional narrator.

When you decide to write in the first person, make sure to introduce your character perfectly. This means that you need to make your readers care about him or her. There are many classic novels that opens the story in this fashion. It can be extremely effective in such a way that the character reaches out to the readers.

You can also begin the story by immediately putting the character in action. That will instantly draw your readers in. Make him do something rather than simply allowing him to describe a past experience or memory.

Another way to create an interesting story in the first person is by introducing a main character who is in the middle of something mysterious or in an intense emotion. This gives the readers an impression that they'll get more from the story if they keep on reading and that there are great revelations they can expect.

Be careful about writing in the first person that's overly close to your own voice. This is a common mistake for many writers. Writing this way can make your character seems like a substitute for your own self. It will appear as one-dimensional. Write about a distinctive character.

Here are a few ways on how to create a unique character for your novel.

- Add a certain personality. Is he an optimistic or pessimistic person? Is she casual or formal in the way she speaks?

- Define the language. Do the characters swear a lot? Does he talk too much or is he a very straightforward person?

- Choose a few words that the character always say, such as "Amazing!" or "That's terrible!" It can serve as an expression when they see things they fancy or hate.

The first person point of view can also be used when introducing your secondary characters in the early part of the story. Although your story starts with the main character's perspective, it doesn't have to limit your focus on the hero alone.

Create a scheme, making your main character mention another character in the opening of your story. That will give your readers something to look forward to as they anticipate the story's progression.

Come up with a plan for your story to make it easier to discover your narrator's voice in the first person point of view.

The Second Person Point of View

When you write in this particular point of view, the narrator basically uses "you" or "your", making the readers the protagonist of the story.

This is rarely used when writing fiction novels, and it is commonly used by non-fiction writers. They say that the second person brings the readers into an instant involvement with the novel through the story's action.

Many writers don't actually recommend using this point of view when writing fiction novels due its level of difficulty. It's quite hard to build the story, as well as your characters, using the second person. It's also difficult to sustain this kind of voice when you're writing a long piece, unlike short pieces, such as an essay.

Developing fictional characters is easier when you're telling a story from their own perspective. Most writers also find it more natural to write in the first or third person since writing in the second person takes so much effort.

There are many reasons why some writers prefer to write in this point of view. One is that they want the readers to experience and feel like the actual protagonist. This is also the best way to capture the readers and fill them with a great sensory experience because it forces them to imagine themselves in that incident. There may also be a certain persuasive passage that they wish to convey that can only be compelling when it's from the second person point of view.

There's absolutely nothing wrong in trying to experiment or explore a specific style of writing. However, writing in the second person takes practice and skill. If you want to be a successful writer in this point of view, it's best to fine-tune your technique.

The Third Person Point of View

This is the most prevalent when it comes to storytelling. Writers use the words "he", "she", "him" or "her" when referring to the character.

Similar to the first person, the third person is also limited to a single character's perspective that serves as its camera. Every detail you add to the story must be seen by the readers through the camera—the character's senses.

There's also the viewpoint called the third person omniscient. The way you refer to the character is still the same, but the storyteller isn't governed by time and writes from a perspective which is all-seeing and all-knowing.

Classic stories brought people up in this kind of narrative, wanting to know every character on and off the stage. They talk about things that are unseen and things that are yet to be seen. For instance, "Little did he know that right around the corner, a stranger awaits him—one who could help turn his life around."

Working on this perspective may appear to be an advantage, yet it is rare for a fiction novel written in this point of view to succeed in the market today. This is mostly employed when writing non-fiction, which makes sense since the writer is trying to convince or educate the readers about a certain topic, telling them everything he knows.

CHOOSING THE BEST POINT OF VIEW

If you've just started out in writing your first novel, you might think that the right voice to use is the first person. But when it comes to modern fiction, the third person is most commonly used by writers.

So what point of view should you really choose? It's still up to you and your objective in writing your novel. But choose wisely. You have to make the readers so engrossed in your story that it's hard for them to put down the book. Your chosen point of view will either make it or break it for you.

Chapter 5: Developing Characters

One of the things that make a novel great is its being character-driven. Someone must always be in the middle of the action. The readers must care about the character that they keep on rooting for him even though he is flawed.

In fact, the character you create should be flawed to make your story relatable and realistic. Besides, no one is perfect—even if you decide that your main character comes from another planet.

When the characters appear real and are highly compelling, readers would want to associate with them more or get intimate with them, welcoming and bringing those character into their world even just for a short time.

Even when the characters seem evil and annoying, they create intrigue and captivate the readers. They want the protagonist to emerge victorious and be transformed—although it still depends on your intention as the writer if your story will end up with the character being triumphant.

HOW TO CREATE THE CHARACTERS

Readers keep on turning the pages when they come across a character who is so much fun to be with. But how do you create a character that readers get to either love or hate?

Again, your research work would come in handy when you're trying to form a truly unpredictable character. Add some details that you've acquired from observing a person, place, or an activity.

The Character Must Be Interesting

A character is the driving force of a novel. If the readers can easily connect with the characters, even if these characters make a lot of mistakes along the way, they will keep on reading because they sympathize with them.

The Hero

But before you dive into writing, you must understand the character first. Your protagonist or the hero of your story, is the most important one. There has to be an arc where the hero goes from being ordinary into a better and phenomenal being.

Your character must possess heroic qualities, which he or she may not even be aware of, that can arise by the time the readers reach the climax.

Don't just create and write about nice characters. Perfect characters are too boring to read. Show the readers that they also have flaws, but their flaws should be justified, or better yet, redeemable.

People don't read novels for the sake of having something good and pleasant to read. They want something that's challenging—perhaps, something that can even challenge their beliefs.

Create complex characters who are good and noble, but not necessarily nice. Fill them with depths and contrasting beliefs. Don't give them a perfect life.

When you write, don't hesitate. Push your characters in order to push your story further to build a compelling world—a world you've never been before.

The Villain

If there's a hero, there's should also be a villain. Just like the protagonist, your antagonist must also be compelling, but daunting. Don't just put a bad guy purely for the sake of having a bad guy in the story. There has to be a reason behind his evil actions and intentions. Give your hero a worthy adversary, someone authentic and memorable.

Of course, the story doesn't solely revolve around the hero and the villain. You also need other regular or recurring characters to form a realistic world.

When you build your set of characters, ask these questions:

- What makes them important in the story?

- What is their goal?

- Who or what keeps them from getting what they want?

- What are they going to do?

Give your characters unique names to make it easier for the readers to distinguish one character from the other. They also have to look and even sound distinct from one another so you won't get the readers confused.

Don't introduce your characters all at the same time or make them present in every scene.

The readers might find it hard to follow the story.

Always remember to add a sense of humanity to every character you write, making them memorable and believable. Readers should feel as if there's a possibility that the characters exist in the real world because they can easily identify with what they're reading. Make them alive in every page of your novel.

Although your hero is strong, smart, noble, or creative, he should also come to a point where he must face his fears and deal with his weaknesses. Your hero must be someone who keeps on improving himself.

For every character you create, list their strengths and weaknesses. It'll be easier for you to make your characters come to life in your novel.

Develop the Character Page

You can start shaping your characters individually by writing a character page. Begin with their physical attributes. Don't make them all look the same. Make them diverse. Just like in the real world, your fantasy world should also show diversity through your characters.

- What does he look like?

- Does she have a straight or curly hair?

- What is the color of his skin?

- Does he have a scar?

- Is she tall or short?

Establish the Backstory

Everybody has a history and even when it comes to history, you must also express diversity. A compelling story should make the readers drawn to the characters.

- Does he come from a rich, middle-class or poor family?

- What is her profession?

- What is his favorite sport?

- What does she like to eat?

- Where does he love to hangout?

Add Some Traits and Habits

Create more engaging characters by building their character traits. These details will help you construct fuller characters that can make them more relatable.

But don't just add little quirks just because you want to. Think about the reason your character possesses a certain trait. This could bring out something interesting out of your story.

- What drives him crazy?

- Does she like fixing or mending broken things?

- Is he always playing with his food before he eats?

- Does she always sit in the back of a bus?

- Does he always forget where he puts his car keys?

Go Deeper With the Characters

Dig deeper when you're creating your characters, particularly your main character. To make them believable and relatable, fashion them after people in the real world. That means they should have worries and problems that they're trying to solve. Maybe there's something bothering them and they don't know what it is or how to handle it.

Show that they, too, have flaws. It's important to make the readers understand them. Even if you're creating characters who come from another part of the galaxy, you can inject some sense of humanity in them that could make the story more interesting.

- Did he experience something traumatic as a child? What is it?

- What makes her heart beat faster?

- What makes him catch his breath?

- What's her childhood like?

- Why does he always wake up at midnight?

Observe What People Do In Real Life

Study real people and then add some of their character traits to your fictional characters. Take note of every detail you see in the real world. Build a set of characters that are truly imaginable.

- What's your brother's weirdest habit?

- What makes your sister very special?

- What can your best friend do that no one else can do?

- What's the craziest thing your roommate ever did?

- What does your colleague love to do that's extremely annoying?

Chapter 6: Designing the Plot

After working on your characters, focus on the actual story, which is the plot. This is the main reason why the readers will pick up your novel in the first place. The plot is what will make them turn every page of your book, so it must be thrilling.

The outline will help you in creating your plot. You must have a clue as to where you want your story to go even though there will be some surprising twists or turn of events along the way.

If you're struggling to think of a great story for your novel, try watching the news or reading some newspapers. You'll see that the truth can be a great source of inspiration, especially when trying to make things up.

Real stories in the real world can be extremely helpful in designing a story's plot. Clearly, you need to put a little twist on the details. Still, it can be a great place to start with.

You must also be keen about writing things you don't really know. Embrace the unknown and allow yourself to make some discoveries, especially for your characters.

Your characters may have skills or expertise that you're not very familiar with. There may be some plot elements which can lead you into strange or unexpected things. Just write them all down and then do the research after.

THE STAKES

When writing your story, there has to be something at risk. The stakes must be high enough to keep your story moving, to keep your characters evolving, and to keep your readers completely engaged.

If the story doesn't have any risk, it will look and feel dull. Your story will lose its pace and your readers won't have enough reasons to keep on turning the pages.

Ask these questions. Is there anything the hero wants to gain or is afraid of losing? What is it and why does it seem so important for him? What is he willing to risk to get what he wants?

Be very clear about what's at stake for your characters in order to make the readers care about their life. Sometimes, there can be many things at risk. Oftentimes, you'll also need to raise the stakes.

Consider a profound conflict when setting personal stakes. Think about several personal stakes that can deeply and immediately influence your main character.

Make sure that when your character makes a choice or decision, there will be consequences. Even when you're writing a fictional story, your characters must still feel like they're alive—breathing and living beings.

That means your hero can't be perfect—he can't always make the right choices. He can't also be invincible—he can't always make the wrong choices without suffering negative consequences.

Look for some ways in which your character will eventually confront the effects and difficulties of every action and decision he makes. Your hero's journey doesn't have to run smoothly. Give his world a little shake.

Keep in mind that your characters don't live in an isolated world. They, too, are part of a larger world and that world is what can bring inspiration to the lives of your readers.

THE CONFLICT

The conflict is what drives a fiction novel. A story without trouble doesn't exist. Even in real life, there's no human being who exists without problems. Whatever genre you're working on for your novel, there has to be a conflict in your story.

A conflict is the beginning of every story. It doesn't matter what part you want to start writing about, remember that your story should establish a conflict at the beginning.

However, that doesn't literally mean that you have to write the conflict on the first sentence or first page of the novel. Let the readers know that the first few pages of the novel will explain the point of the story.

Give the hero a moral predicament. Compel him to choose between something detestable to him and detestable to others.

Once you've captured your readers' interest with a gripping opening and gave your hero a problem to overcome, make him want to save himself from all the trouble yet ends up making things worse. Many writers make the mistake of making their hero's life way too simple.

For instance, instead of giving your hero a perfect girlfriend, a nice house or apartment, a good job, or a private car, take everything that makes life comfortable away from him.

You can write about his girlfriend cheating on him, his house destroyed by an unexpected storm, get him suddenly fired from his job, or get his car stolen from him. Place him in a disastrous or dangerous situation.

But you have to be careful when writing about your character's weaknesses. Don't make him appear foolish. Your hero may have certain flaws, but those flaws should be redeemable and notable rather than hateful or annoying.

Make the problem more intense but in a logical sense because of the main character's efforts in trying to resolve things. You can imply that he's growing and progressing, which will bring him success by the end of the story, but make his trouble increase immensely.

Think about the moment your main character hits rock bottom. That will either be a make it or break it opportunity for you as a writer.

Your writing voyage will not be easy. Giving your hero a rest, creating an escape, or placing a miracle sounds tempting, but you have to resist.

When your hero experiences the most miserable moment of his life, he'll be forced to do something—using every muscle and ability that he has gained from all of the obstacles he has faced only to discover that things are already beyond repair.

Making your hero's circumstances more desperate and dreadful will open a path that leads to a more powerful climax and resolution.

You have to consider what will be the conflict of your story. Remember that a compelling fiction novel has conflict. You can create whatever conflict you want for your story—a broken family, a forsaken relationship, a brutal murder, a teenager trying to find his true identity, an old person who is still attempting to pursue his greatest dream.

Then determine the way you want the conflict to be settled.

THE CLIMAX

The highest point of action right before your story ends is the climax. It is where your story's conflict must somehow be concluded. It is the final resolution—the part that can be completely emotional. It's when the hero must ultimately face the greatest test. It's a do or die situation.

When working on the climax, remember to add some twists and turns. Surprise your readers. That will make your fiction novel absolutely engrossing.

They say that if you fail to surprise yourself with your story, then you won't be able to surprise your readers either.

Some writers argue that a story ought to come to a climax at the end, but what they actually mean is that the story should be at its highest point on the last few pages or the closing act. But when your story is built around a tremendous fantasy world, the climax should be written in the last chapters of the book.

What you create can either turn into success or turn into a disaster. Even when you establish a strong emotion towards the end of the story, you have to make sure that your readers can completely grasp what would come next. Otherwise, you'll only leave them feeling confused and deceived.

Still, it all boils down to what is best for your novel. You can opt not to place an important moment at the end and perfectly give your readers a surprise ending, but you have to do it the right way.

The climax can be the most amazing, exciting, or even upsetting moment in the story. You have to give your readers the outcome they've been waiting for. Reward them for sticking with your story by giving them a satisfying ending of a hero's journey. Leave them with one of the most fulfilling experiences just by reading your novel.

Keep in mind that your story doesn't end with the climax. The ending is yet to come.

Chapter 7: Ending the Story

A great ending is well-thought out. It awakens the readers' emotions, such as delight, sadness, or anger. It brings inspiration to the readers and it can completely change their perspective. Most importantly, it respects the readers because they have invested their time and money just to keep on turning the pages until the very end.

The narrative of a great story doesn't end in deceit. The hero, together with the readers, is brought to a certain destination—and it doesn't matter whether they end up trapped or victorious.

The ending gives emphasis to the way a character has transformed from the start of the story. If your character ends up being exactly the same as he was before, then your story needs a serious character progression, which is a crucial aspect in writing fiction. You'll have to go through the revision stage.

In order to avoid a total revision for your story, you need to know how you can create a good ending for your entire narrative.

It's also important not to allow the ending to simply die out due to an extremely dramatic climax. Although the ending will not be action-filled or dramatic like the climax, it still needs to be captivating, or even controversial.

You should be able to complete the whole hero's journey at the end with an emotional strike. Don't rush when writing the ending. Take some time to write a completely satisfying ending.

DIFFERENT TYPES OF ENDING

Straight-Up or Linear Ending

When your main character has accomplished his pursuit, his journey has now come to an end. He starts to move on after learning everything he had to know. You can choose to make this a happy or sad ending, or even somewhere in between the two. There are countless romantic stories, dramas and adventures that end in this manner.

Cliffhanger

You're probably familiar with what this type of ending implies. It doesn't totally provide the readers with a complete ending. The hero is left in the middle of an unresolved problem or danger. TV shows and movies often employ this kind of ending—the end of a particular chapter in the story. In novels, open endings where it's up to the readers' imagination to think about the hero's fate, falls under this category.

A Shocking Revelation

An ending like this usually leaves the readers in total surprise. They don't expect that there's going to be one final twist to the story, leaving them in awe. Endings like these can change the understanding of the readers in terms of the story's events. Stories under the genre of horror and thrillers commonly use this type of ending.

The Thinker

Do you want your readers to be left in wonder but not completely hanging? This could be a great kind of ending for your novel. You simply invite the readers to ponder and look into the essence of the story. The journey of your hero may come to an end, but there's still more to it.

A Dreadful Ending

As much as you can, avoid writing a dreadful ending for your novel. These are endings where the readers will realize that the hero of the story is really insane, or that everything that happened in the story was just a dream or an illusion. It's not really wrong to create an ending like this; you just have to do it remarkably well.

HOW TO WRITE A GREAT ENDING

Start With the Ending

Many writers prefer to begin their novel by working on the ending first. If you're aware as to where your story is going, it'll be a lot easier and faster for you to reach the end. Make an outline beginning with the ending and then work on the entire story. Awful endings tend to end up that way because novelists write them right then and there, not having a clue as to where the story will eventually lead into.

Write Different Endings

Even filmmakers produce several endings for a particular movie. You can do the same with your novel. Write various alternatives for your ending. Make your hero end up in another circumstance. You can give him a happy, gloomy, decisive or unresolved ending. Eventually, it will lead you towards an ending that will appear to be the best among all of your options and one that best works for your story.

Remember that it doesn't matter whether you write something emotional, clever, or eccentric, what matters is that your story has a heart.

Do Some Research for Different Endings

Grab a bundle of books, but don't read everything—just the first and last section. Though it may spoil things for you, you'll get a bunch of ideas from other authors. See which endings are effective and which endings don't work.

Wrap Things Up

It's not only the journey of the hero that you need to wrap up, you should also wrap up everything else that might be lying around. It's the point where you need to make certain that you don't leave any open plot holes or leave with your characters being lost, needing an explanation. Don't let these details get discovered after your novel gets published.

Find an Honest Reader

It's extremely helpful to have an honest, though cruel, test reader beside you. Test readers can inform you if you have chosen the right ending for your story. There's no better way in telling whether the ending of your story is riveting or horrible than hearing it from a direct and truthful reader.

Give Important to the Last Line

See to it that your hero is present until the very last word of your novel. The final line is what brings an excellent punch to the readers—sticking with them even after putting down the book. Go over your pile of books and read their last lines to get some good ideas.

THINGS TO BEAR IN MIND

There is a perfect moment to bring your story to its end. As the writer, it's important for you to understand when it's already time to stop.

Many writers often send a rough draft where they only end up repeating previous actions, going towards a new but irrelevant detour. This only shows that you didn't take enough time to create an outline to know where the story should go.

However, don't end your story too early as well. Be cautious of ending it in an untimely manner that causes you to leave your storyline still unexplained.

When you're writing a thriller or mystery novel, it would be a crime not to solve the secrets and puzzles for your readers.

Again, your story doesn't have to end up being happy, inspiring, or successful—unless you want it to which is a good thing. What really matters in writing a novel is to make the hero overcome various obstacles, leaving him, as well as the readers, with a phenomenal experience and real wisdom to acquire.

Endings are really all about change. It would be very disappointing for the readers to turn towards the last page of the book, realizing that the hero and all the other characters remain the same throughout the story.

Make things happen. Fiction and even non-fiction stories deal with the overcoming of crucial obstacles, search, and transformations. You don't necessarily have to write about good changes. In fact, your story can be sad or depressing. Yet, if your characters weren't able to learn anything after all of the challenges they have faced in the story, your novel will be unsatisfying, pointless, and will have no meaning at all.

Always end your story with a proper resolution. Remember that your conflict can only be settled through resolution. Provide one that ends on positive note—a meaningful message that your readers can take with them.

Great stories help break down many barriers and remove the noise surrounding the readers. When you make your story's experience personal, people will have a greater connection to it, which will ultimately lead to your novel's success.

Remember that as a writer, it is your job to stir the right emotions and establish relationships right from the very beginning.

Try to really understand your readers in order to create an innate experience, increasing the challenges and creating mental conflict. But unless you settle the conflict and make your readers feel empowered to face their own demons, your story is not yet complete.

Guide your readers on an adventure. Keep them hooked until you get to tell them what they need to do next. When the right time comes, allow other people to narrate the story.

Chapter 8: Asking For Feedback

The moment you write the final words for the ending, take a break and then go through your entire novel. Check if there are some typos, spelling mistakes, awkward sentences, or grammatical errors.

You might still discover some plot holes throughout your story. Look for weird transitions or see if there's any part that seems boring. Continue to work on them to fix them.

If you're confident enough about your work, it's time for you to find someone who can read your work. It has to be someone you completely trust.

Many writers who are just starting out make the biggest mistake of immediately showing their work to anyone. It can be appealing, especially when you're seeking a feedback after writing your first novel. Maybe you're eager to show how proud you are of your work. But before you do anything, hit pause. Think about what can happen when you let so many people read your novel at an early point in time.

People will definitely give you all kinds of ideas once they've read your story. They'll tell you what they think is the best angle, what path to follow, what to add or even what to edit out. You have to keep in mind that at the end of the day, it's still your story.

THINGS YOU SHOULDN'T DO

First, never post your story pages on your social media accounts, such as Facebook and Twitter, and then ask for feedback. This has never worked with any novelists before. It will surely end up in a disaster and you'll hate yourself for doing it.

Think about it this way. It's just like going to a park and standing in a spot while asking random people who pass by what they think about the way you look. Now, can you see the picture?

Second, don't argue with people when they give a feedback for your novel. Don't tell them that they don't understand what you're trying to say in your story. It's just like insulting their judgment or disposition. After all, they will surely have different opinions from you.

Third, when they criticize your book, that doesn't mean they're criticizing you. Never make that mistake, especially with the experts. They only want you to succeed in your career as a novelist, which is why they'll strive to be as honest as possible when it comes to your work.

Lastly, don't ignore other people's feedback. Why would you ask for it in the first place if you'll only dismiss their opinion? Listen to what they have to say, but you don't have to take in everything they say.

THINGS YOU SHOULD DO

Find a Mentor

Look for someone who has already done what you're trying to do and ask from some useful advice or feedback. There's always a person who's willing to mentor you and help you save a lot of time from pitfalls and errors.

It's better to find a mentor who's really knowledgeable in the writing or publishing industry. It can be another writer or an editor. He might know how to get in touch with agents and publishers.

There are many people out there who can deceive you because they think highly of themselves but never produced anything successfully at all. Just because someone writes a bunch of emails every day, it doesn't make them an appropriate critic. Be careful whom you're entrusting your work with. Still, you can find plenty of writing experts out there.

You Can Consider Asking Your Friends and Family

You can let your family and friends read your novel and ask what they think could be the boring parts of the story. You then might have to cut out a few chunks to further improve your work.

However, also be cautious when asking them for some feedback. Since they're your family and friends, they might try to say nice things about your story, which can ruin your work. Unless your friend or family member is an expert on the field, don't try to agree with everything they say.

Writing takes time. Build your vision and put it on the page. There's a right time to allow and accept other people's opinions to improve your work. Remember that there are writers who love collaborating to produce great novels, but there's no novel that's written by a whole bunch of people.

Spend quality time with your novel. Once you're completely sure of what you want to do and you understand the whole process, then find a group or join a class to refine your work.

They key to further develop your novel is to ask certain people—people who are experts in what you do or know your audience very well.

Seek specific feedback from specific people. Don't let your time and effort be wasted from trying to ask random people about your work. Trust your work and let the experts guide you. In the end, what's important is the story you want to tell as a writer.

Conclusion

I'd like to thank you and congratulate you for transiting my lines from start to finish.

I hope this book was able to help you to get started on your fiction novel. Writing can be a daunting task, but it's also an enjoyable process as you get to know more about the real world and your fantasy world—captivating your readers by means of writing something they can relate to.

The next step is to keep on writing until you find your own voice as a writer. Create your world, foster it, and it will surely make your readers drawn to every page of your book.

What did you think of, **How To Write A Novel: Simple Steps to Write Compelling Novels That Keep The Pages Turning**

I know you could have picked any number of books to read, but you picked this book and for that I am extremely grateful. I hope that it added at value and quality to your everyday life. If so, it would be really nice if you could share this book with your friends and family by posting to Facebook and Twitter.

If you enjoyed this book and found some benefit in reading this, I'd like to hear from you and hope that you could take some time to post a review. Your feedback and support will help this author to greatly improve his writing craft for future projects and make this book even better. I want you, the reader, to know that your review is very important and so, if you'd like to leave a review, all you have to do is click here and away you go.

I wish you all the best in your future success!

William Swain

Unlock Your True Writing Potential

What's holding back your writing? Take this free assessment now and learn to unlock your true potential:

https://www.subscribepage.com/novel